A BEGINNER'S GUIDE TO THE STOCK MARKET

MATTHEW R. KRATTER

WWW.TRADER.UNIVERSITY

CONTENTS

For my wife and children

DISCLAIMER

Neither Little Cash Machines LLC, nor any of its directors, officers, shareholders, personnel, representatives, agents, or independent contractors (collectively, the "Operator Parties") are licensed financial advisers, registered investment advisers, or registered broker-dealers. None of the Operator Parties are providing investment, financial, legal, or tax advice, and nothing in this book or at www.trader.university (henceforth, "the Site") should be construed as such by you. This book and the Site should be used as educational tools only and are not replacements for professional investment advice.

The full disclaimer may be found at the end of this book.

YOUR FREE GIFT

Thanks for buying my book!

To show my appreciation, I would like to send you a **FREE BONUS BOOK**, which contains 3 chapters:

- **"Interview with a Millionaire Trader"** (how he got started, and which trading strategies he is using today)
- **"Best Online Stock Screeners"** (my favorite stock scanners that I use to screen for momentum stocks and other trading set-ups)
- **"The Fastest Way to Grow a Small Trading Account"** (if you are trading less than $5,000, you won't want to miss this chapter)

To get your FREE copy of this book, tap here now:

>>>Tap Here to Get Your Free Bonus Chapter<<<

Or simply go to:

https://www.trader.university/beginners-guide-bonus

THE WORLD'S GREATEST OPPORTUNITY MACHINE

The stock market is the greatest opportunity machine ever created.

I believe that everyone should have access to the stock market, not just the rich and privileged. That's why I wrote this book.

There is a place for everyone and every strategy in the stock market. You can invest in stocks, holding them for many years and pocketing their dividends.

You can also trade stocks. You can day trade them, swing trade them, or short them (bet that a stock is going to go down instead of up). Don't ever let anyone tell you what you can or cannot do with stocks. After reading this book, you may even come up with your own original way of profiting from the stock market that no one has ever used before.

In this book, I will give you an overview of many different approaches to the stock market. When you are first getting started, you should try out many different trading and investing strategies and see what works for you.

Each one of us has a different psychological make-up and approach to risk. Some love the quick dopamine hits that come from trading. Others just want to live their lives, and get rich slowly and quietly without any stress. There is room for both types of people in the stock market.

I would just urge you to learn how the stock market *actually* works. Many people never take the time to learn this. Many people like to yell at the stock market and tell it what to do.

The stock market is a complex emergent system. It won't listen to you or to anyone else. It's like the weather-- it just does what it does, so you might as well get used to it. Take the time to learn how the stock market *really* works.

This is important because we live in a world driven by financial markets. If you can learn even a little bit about how they work, you can give yourself a huge advantage in life.

To repeat what I said at the beginning of this book:

The stock market is the greatest opportunity machine ever created.

Unfortunately, most people never learn how to harness its energy to create wealth.

You are clearly not like most people.

You purchased this book because something in the title, cover, or book description resonated with you.

I believe that you are destined for something greater. You know that trading and investing are skills that can actually be learned. And you are ready to put in the time and effort to make that happen. That makes you my ideal kind of reader. I want to help you to get rich.

The stock market has been really good to me and my family. I'm at the point where my biggest goal is to give back. That's why for the last few years, I have been teaching others how to trade and invest through my books and courses at https://www.trader.university/.

So read this book slowly, and let its lessons sink in. Read it again after you've had your first big losing trade. Or just read it whenever you need a little inspiration.

You can also subscribe to my YouTube channel and follow along as I tell you what I'm seeing in the markets every week:

https://www.youtube.com/c/traderuniversity

I hope that you find this book helpful. I wrote it for the person who knows little or nothing about the stock market, but has the intellectual curiosity and hunger to learn.

So let's get started!

What exactly is a stock anyway?

A stock is a share of ownership in a company. When I buy 100 shares of McDonald's, I become a partial owner of the company. I become a "shareholder." If I had enough cash, I could simply buy up every share of McDonald's, and then I would own the entire company. I would be the emperor of burgers.

Here's another way to think about it. McDonald's is like a pie that has 765,317,332 slices (shares outstanding). As I am typing these words, each of these slices is valued by the market at $187.62. That's what we mean when we say that the stock is trading at 187.62.

Now let's take the total number of slices and multiply it by the price per slice. We get about $143.58 billion. That's the current total value of this "pie" that we call McDonald's. Another word for this is "market cap" or "market capitalization."

When we hear that Apple has become the biggest company in the world, we usually mean that it has the highest market cap. On 3 October 2018, Apple had a market cap of $1.103 trillion. Today (20 May 2019), its market cap is $840 billion.

A company's stock price and market cap will move around a lot over time. This is because all of the world's smartest minds (and computers) are constantly processing new information and collectively deciding what a company is worth.

By buying or selling a company's stock, these traders and investors push a stock's price to where it should be trading based on all known information about the company.

Sometimes the market is temporarily wrong. In 1999, Pets.com was valued at about $300 million. A year later, it was valued at zero, as the company went out of business.

In 1996, Apple was valued at less than $3 billion. Then the company brought back Steve Jobs, who introduced the iPod and the iPhone. The price of Apple's stock (and hence its market cap) first slowly (and then quickly) ramped up as the market began to figure out how successful and profitable these devices would be.

The stock market adjusts to new information. That is one thing that makes stocks wiggle around. Stocks also move based on the laws of supply and demand. If a lot of people want to buy a stock, the share price will move up. Maybe those people are overly optimistic, but their buying will still cause the stock to move up. Then if a very large investor comes in and starts to dump his stock, the price of the stock will move down.

Sometimes it is a mystery why a stock is trading up or down. Eventually it becomes apparent. Legendary hockey player Wayne Gretzky is famous for saying:

I skate to where the puck is going to be, not to where it has been.

The stock market does something similar. It tries to figure out what is most likely to happen over the next 3-6 months, and then prices stocks accordingly. That's why we say that the stock market is a "forward-looking mechanism" or "discounting mechanism."

In early 2009, the U.S. economy was still in really bad shape. Everyone was still losing their homes and jobs. Even so, the stock market began to move up off of its lows. Then it really began to rally. This confused a lot of people who were looking out of their windows and still seeing bad economic conditions. But what the stock market was doing was pricing in an economic recovery, which turned out to be correct.

The same kind of thing can happen with an individual stock. Sometimes a stock will report great earnings (i.e. tell everyone that it had a good quarter and made a lot of money), but still fall sharply the next day. It does this because traders are reacting to something else in the earnings call or in management's forward-looking statements. The stock is "skating" to where the company is going to be in a few months.

An inexperienced trader will be tempted to buy a stock like

this when it is down, but this is almost always a bad idea. It can take time for new information to get priced into a stock, which means that this stock could continue to move lower for days or even weeks.

The reverse can also happen. A company may report much higher than expected earnings. The next day, the stock gaps up (opens up much higher than where it was trading the previous day). Then the stock continues to move higher for a few days, or even weeks.

This happens because the big institutional players (mutual funds, pensions, hedge funds) are buying more shares of the stock and driving it closer to its new "fair value" price based on the new information that came out in the earnings report and call. When one is buying millions (or even billions) of dollars worth of stock, as these players are, one cannot do it simply by pressing a button. It can take hours, days, or even weeks.

In a later chapter, I am going to show you how you can make money by taking advantage of these slow, lumbering giants. But for now, I'd like to stick to the basics.

In the next chapter, I will show you how to open up a brokerage account and buy your first stock.

2

HOW TO GET STARTED WITH STOCKS

Some people like to buy stocks and hold them for many years. We call them "investors."

Other people like to buy and sell stocks more quickly, maybe holding them for only an hour, a day, a week, or a month. We call these people "traders."

Both are perfectly good ways to make money in the stock market. Some investors look down on traders, and vice versa. I would urge you not to take a side in this debate.

I am both a trader and an investor. I like to have many different strategies running at the same time: long-term strategies, short-term strategies, as well as strategies that involve bonds, options, futures, currencies, venture capital, and real estate. You should try the different strategies that I describe in this book, in order to discover what works best for you and your personal psychology and risk tolerance.

Remember to consult with a registered financial adviser before making any investment decisions.

Then when you are ready, the question will arise:

So how exactly do I buy a stock?

Stocks are usually bought and sold on what are called "stock exchanges." A stock exchange is simply a place where buyers and sellers show up and exchange their shares for money, or their money for shares. A stock exchange is a little bit like an eBay for stocks.

The most well-known exchanges in the U.S. are the New York Stock Exchange (NYSE) and the Nasdaq. The NYSE is best known for its blue chip (high-quality) stocks like Coca-Cola and McDonald's. The Nasdaq is best known for its tech stocks like Netflix and Apple.

NYSE stocks are usually identified by a two-letter unique "ticker" (stock symbol) like KO (Coca-Cola) or HD (Home Depot). Nasdaq stocks usually have four-letter tickers like AAPL (Apple) or NFLX (Netflix). Occasionally you'll also find a two-letter ticker on the NASDAQ like FB (Facebook).

Stock exchanges used to involve a lot of men standing on a floor with little pads of paper and yelling buy and sell orders. Now it's all done by computers. The computers match up buyers and sellers who want to exchange their stock for cash (or vice versa) at a certain price.

As an individual, you cannot trade directly on a stock exchange. For that you will need a "broker" or "brokerage account." A broker is simply a middleman who gives people access to a stock exchange. In the U.S., well-known brokers include Charles Schwab, Interactive Brokers, TD Ameritrade, TradeStation, Fidelity, and E*Trade.

My favorite broker is Robinhood.com. They make it really easy for beginners. You go to their website, fill out some online paperwork, then move some money into your newly opened brokerage account. Robinhood.com is great because they allow you to buy and sell stocks without paying a commission (fee).

Once you've opened up your brokerage account, it's time to buy your first stock. I've created a video here that will show you how to do it on Robinhood:

https://www.trader.university/buy-stocks-robinhood

When you are buying a stock, you will be given the choice of using two different kinds of orders. The first is called a "market order." This order tells the broker to get you into the stock as quickly as possible, regardless of price. If you use a market order, you might end up buying the stock at a price that is far away from where it last traded.

This is because every stock has a bid price and an offer (or "ask") price. The bid is the price at which someone is willing to buy the stock. The offer is the price at which someone is willing to sell the stock. Memorize this phrase right now:

"You sell to the bid, and you buy from the ask."

The distance between the bid and the ask is called the "bid-ask spread." A liquid stock like Microsoft (MSFT) or Apple (AAPL) will have a bid-ask spread of just a penny. So right now as I'm writing these words, there is someone at the bid for Microsoft who is willing to buy 2,200 shares for 120.25. And there is someone at the ask who is willing to sell 1,200 shares for 120.26. That's a bid-ask spread of just a penny ($0.01).

A liquid stock is defined as a stock where you can buy or sell a lot of shares without moving the stock too much. Liquid stocks in the U.S. usually have a bid-ask spread of just a penny or two.

If you place a market order to buy a liquid stock, you will usually be OK. That's because a market order will tell the broker that you want to buy your shares from the ask. Since it is just a penny away from the bid price, your order will usually be filled very close to where you are currently seeing the stock trade.

However, if you use a market order on an illiquid stock, you might get a price that is far away from the current market, or from where the stock last traded.

Let's say that stock XYZ is illiquid. There's a bid for just 300 shares at 50.00. And there's an ask for just 200 shares at 52.00. If you use a market order on a stock like this, you will have your order filled at 52.00 or higher.

If you place a market order for 400 shares on XYZ, your broker will first give you the 200 shares at 52.00. Then it will look for the next best price. In an illiquid stock, that might be another 100 shares at 52.25 and then another 100 shares at 52.50. So you will end up getting 400 shares of XYZ at an average price of 52.1875.

Now let's say that you made a mistake and want to immediately sell your stock. If you place a market order to sell, you will first be able to sell 300 shares to the bid at 50.00. Then maybe the next highest bid is 100 shares at 49.50. If you are filled at these prices, you will end up having lost $925 (before commission), even though the stock has not really moved.

That is why it is usually best to stay away from illiquid stocks. If you absolutely must trade them, you can try putting in a limit order that is right in the middle of the bid-ask spread. But there is no guarantee that your order will ever be filled.

A limit order is the second type of order, after a market order. Whereas a market order tells your broker to just get you into or out of the stock as fast as possible, a limit order specifies a price. So if you place a limit order to buy MSFT at 120.25, your order will only be filled if there is a seller that is willing to part with the shares at that price. If there is never a seller at that price, your order will never be filled.

I almost always use limit orders in my trading, even with highly liquid stocks. So if I want to buy a liquid stock like Microsoft, I will look where the ask is, and then just enter a limit order using that ask price. That way I won't get into trouble if a bit of market-moving news comes out one millisecond after I place my order and Microsoft suddenly spikes to 126. In this situation, if you have used a market order, there is a good chance that you will get filled at 126, even though Microsoft is a liquid stock.

When you place an order to buy or sell a stock, you will have one more choice to make:

"Do I use a Day order or a GTC order?"

A Day order will only be executed during regular market hours today. If the order has not been filled by the time the stock market closes for the day, it will be automatically cancelled by the broker.

A GTC ("good 'til cancelled") order will be good for today's market hours, as well as the following days and weeks. If you don't cancel it, it will still be working. Some brokers will automatically cancel a GTC order after a month or more, if it has not yet been filled. Check with your particular broker to find out their policies.

Normal trading hours for U.S. stock exchanges like the NYSE and Nasdaq are 9:30 am EST to 4 pm EST. Some brokers will let you trade stocks in the pre-market trading session (4 am to 9:30 am EST) or in the post-market trading session (also known as "after-hours trading" and lasting from 4 pm to 8 pm EST).

If you are going to trade before the market opens or in the after-hours market, always use a limit order.

Even normally liquid stocks can be quite illiquid (and hence volatile) during both of these trading sessions. "Volatile" means that the stock wiggles around or jumps around a lot. You may see it trading at 85, then 87, then 82, then back to 85. Stocks with lower trading volume will usually be more volatile, with a wide bid-ask spread that also bounces around.

Until you become an advanced trader, it is probably best to stick to normal market hours. And please don't ever trade an IPO using market orders. That is the ultimate newbie mistake. More on that in a later chapter...

3

MAKE MONEY WITH ETF'S

N ow that you've opened up a brokerage account, you are ready to buy your first stock. Which stock should you buy?

Many investors choose to buy an index, rather than a single stock. An index is simply a collection (or "basket") of stocks. Let's say that we take the 500 U.S. stocks with the largest market caps and toss them into a big basket. That basket is called the S&P 500.

(Technical note: indices like the S&P 500 are market-cap weighted, which means that the companies in them that have larger market caps are given higher weightings and thus have a greater influence on the index. If Apple has a bad day, the S&P 500 will go down more than if the Campbell Soup

Company has a bad day. You can see the relative weightings here:

https://www.slickcharts.com/sp500

You've probably also heard of 2 other indices (plural for "index").

There's the Dow Jones Industrial Average (DJIA). This is a famous index that goes back to 1896. It always contains only 30 companies. Sometimes a company gets kicked out, and a new company added. This recently happened to General Electric, which was kicked out and replaced by Walgreens. When you hear on the news that the "Dow" was down 300 points, this is the index that is being referred to.

The 30 Dow stocks are usually very large and well-known companies. Sometimes people call them "blue chips" or "blue chip stocks" because they are large, mature, profitable, and fairly stable companies. To see which stocks are currently in the Dow, you can go here:

https://en.wikipedia.org/wiki/
Dow_Jones_Industrial_Average#Components

Another well-known index is the Nasdaq 100, which contains mostly tech companies. You can see its current components here:

https://en.wikipedia.org/wiki/NASDAQ-100#Components

Most Nasdaq 100 companies can be considered "blue-chip companies" as well.

If you wanted to invest in an index like the S&P 500, you would need to buy all 500 stocks at the same time. That would be difficult and costly to execute. Fortunately, there is an easier way to do it.

Some smart people came up with the idea of the ETF ("exchange-traded fund"). An ETF trades just like a stock. You can buy or sell it all day long in your brokerage account. Each ETF represents a certain index. So the ETF for the S&P 500 trades under the ticker SPY. The ETF for the DJIA trades under the ticker DIA. And the ETF for the Nasdaq 100 trades under the ticker QQQ.

You've probably heard of the QQQ. It is a great trading or investment vehicle. When you buy shares of the QQQ, you are getting exposure to Apple, Netflix, Google, Amazon, Facebook, and many other tech (and some non-tech) stocks. If you buy the QQQ and hold it for the long-term, you will be able to profit from the long-term growth of the tech industry.

You've probably also heard of indexing. It consists of buying an index (usually using an ETF like the SPY or QQQ), and holding it for the long-term. Indexing is a form of "passive investing." Passive investing refers to any strategy that does not involve a lot of thinking ("which stocks should I buy today?") or a lot of buying or selling.

When you index, you just buy whatever stocks are in the index. You only sell a stock when it gets kicked out of the index. And you only buy a stock when it gets added to the index. Or you just buy the SPY or QQQ, and these index adjustments all get done automatically for you.

Today indexing is widely considered the safest and best way for most people to invest in the stock market. If you own the S&P 500 index, you are basically guaranteed to get the same long-term return of the U.S. large-cap stock market, less investment expenses.

In the old days, very few people practiced indexing. That guaranteed that it would provide pretty good returns. These days, anywhere from 50-70% of the money in the stock market is tied to indexing. This almost certainly ensures that investment returns will not be as good in the future as they have been in the past.

That being said, most people lose money when they try to trade or invest on their own, so they will still be better off pursuing an indexing strategy. That's because *active* investing strategies (as opposed to *passive* investing strategies like indexing) are difficult. Most people don't invest in learning the necessary skills to do it well.

When indexing, most people like to invest the same dollar amount of money into an index every month. That way, you never buy all of your stock at the very top of the market. By buying a stock or index/ETF at different times, you are allowing the wiggles of the stock to smooth themselves out, since you are always buying at a different price. By doing this, you end up getting a pretty good "average price." That is why this practice is called "cost averaging."

Another way to index is to buy a low-cost mutual fund like the Vanguard 500, which only charges you an expense ratio (annual fee) equal to 0.04% of your investment. By comparison, the SPY ETF charges a 0.0945% expense ratio, but allows you to trade in and out of the stock during the day. Mutual funds like the Vanguard 500 only allow you to buy or sell shares once a day based on closing market prices.

Most investors are probably better off starting with the SPY, since you can invest as little as a few hundred dollars. Currently, to invest in the Vanguard 500 mutual fund, you will need to have at least $3,000.

Buying a stock index like the S&P 500 is a great way to get started investing. If you can, you should just buy some SPY and not look at it for the next 30 years. When you are indexing, it doesn't make any sense to check daily stock or index prices.

That being said, a great time to invest in an index like the S&P 500 is during a bear market. If stock prices have been falling for 6 months or more, and there is a lot of pessimism in the air, it might be a good time to invest some extra money into index funds. This is because lower stock prices will allow you to buy more shares of stock for the same dollar amount than you could if stock prices were higher.

Now that we have covered indexing, it is time to turn to dividend investing.

4

CREATING PASSIVE INCOME WITH DIVIDEND STOCKS

dividend stock will usually make a cash payment into your brokerage account every 3 months. That cash payment is called a dividend.

Investing in dividend stocks is one of the best ways to build wealth. The reason it works so well is that you can take the cash from a dividend payment and use it to buy more dividend stocks. Then those dividend stocks will pay you more dividends.

If you keep doing this over many years, you will end up like Ronald Read. He spent the first half of his life as a gas station attendant, and the second half of his life as a janitor at a J.C. Penney department store. He lived a simple, frugal life and funneled much of his earnings into dividend stocks. When he died at the age of 92, he left behind an $8 million fortune, all in dividend stocks.

It's a good reminder that you don't need to have a high salary to become a millionaire. You just need to spend less than you earn, and invest the rest in dividend stocks.

When you own dividend stocks, the cash hits your brokerage account every 3 months, whether you have a job or not. It's a little bit like owning a rental property, except that you never need to go over to fix the toilet. The best thing about dividend stocks is that the management and the employees of the company do all of the work, while you get to sit around and collect dividend checks.

Let's say that you buy a dividend stock XYZ at $60 per share that pays you $0.45 every 3 months (quarterly):

$0.45 paid 4 times every year is $1.80. That's your annual total in dividends.

Now take $1.80 divided by the price that you paid for the stock ($60):

$1.80/$60 is 0.03 or 3%.

3% is what we call the stock's "dividend yield." If you put your money in a savings account, you might make 2% every year. That is your savings account's yield.

Expressing things in terms of yield allows us to compare

different investments. In this case, the dividend stock has a higher yield than the savings account, which is a good thing. However, when you buy a stock, it can always go down in price and lose you money. That doesn't happen with a savings account.

A successful company will raise its dividend every year. Let's say that the imaginary company mentioned above raises its dividend every year by 7.2%. After 10 years of doing this, the annual dividend payment will have doubled, from $1.80 to $3.60. You paid just $60 for each share of stock, so now your dividend yield is 6% (3.60/60). The longer you hold a dividend stock like this, the higher your effective yield becomes.

Warren Buffett bought Coke in 1988. His effective dividend yield today on those original shares is over 60%. In other words, he now receives more in Coke dividends every 1.7 years than the grand total that he paid for his original shares. That's one reason that the man is a billionaire.

Coke is a special kind of dividend stock. It is a Dividend Aristocrat, one of an elite group of companies that have raised their dividends every year for the past 25 years. Other Dividend Aristocrats include the Colgate-Palmolive Company, Johnson & Johnson, and McDonald's.

There's an easy way to own a piece of every Dividend Aristocrat: just buy some shares of NOBL. It is the ProShares S&P

500 Dividend Aristocrats ETF. It trades just like a stock, and you can purchase it using any brokerage account.

Wondering how much a company (like Apple) pays in dividends?

Just head over to Google and type in: "How much does Apple pay in dividends?"

In order to pay a dividend, a company needs to be making money itself. Occasionally a company will borrow money to pay its dividend, but that can never last for very long.

Dividends are usually paid out of a company's free cash flow. One of the great things about investing in dividend stocks is that you know that the company is making money. Otherwise it wouldn't be able to pay you every three months.

Owning a basket of dividend stocks over a long period of time is one of the best ways to build wealth.

If you start early enough, you may even end up with millions like Ronald Read.

5

HOW TO PICK STOCKS LIKE WARREN BUFFETT

W henever I hear Warren Buffett talk about his investing strategy, he always makes it seem so easy. You just buy a wonderful company at a fair price and hold it for the next 50 years.

It seems like anyone could have seen that Coca-Cola was going to be a grand slam. But how many people do you know who have owned Coca-Cola since 1988 (which is when Buffett bought it)?

Hindsight is 20/20. But in the world of investments, we are forced to think about the future. Investing like Buffett is hard. You need to pick companies that are going to be around (and continuing to do well) in 20 years from now. And you must be careful not to overpay for them.

Those are not easy things to do. Even Warren Buffett occasionally makes a mistake here, as he recently admitted to overpaying for Kraft-Heinz.

That being said, there's a really easy way to pick stocks like Warren Buffett:

Just copy him.

Go here and download his letter for the most recent year:

http://www.berkshirehathaway.com/letters/letters.html

Scroll down and you will see a list of every stock that Buffett owns. For the 2018 letter, you can find this list on page 12 of the PDF. It includes the following stocks:

American Express (AXP)

Apple (AAPL)

Bank of America (BAC)

Bank of New York Mellon (BK)

Charter Communications (CHTR)

The Coca-Cola Company (KO)

Delta Air Lines (DAL)

Goldman Sachs (GS)

JPMorgan Chase (JPM)

Moody's (MCO)

Southwest Airlines (LUV)

United Continental Holdings (UAL)

U.S. Bancorp (USB)

USG Corporation (USG)

Wells Fargo (WFC)

One of the coolest things about this list is that you can use it to calculate the average price that Buffett paid for each stock. Just take the "cost" for each stock and divide it by the "number of shares."

Buffett has held most of these stocks for many years, so you probably won't get a chance to purchase any of them at his prices. That being said, occasionally one of his new picks will fall below his purchase price, and you will have the opportunity to purchase some shares at a lower price than Buffett himself paid. I've done that a few times over the years.

You could also just buy a basket of these stocks that Buffett owns. Buy the basket of stocks, and then sell a stock only when you hear that Buffett has exited the position.

An even easier route might be to just buy some B-shares of Berkshire Hathaway (ticker: BRK-B). One share of stock in this company will cost you $203.27 today. You can then sit back and relax and let Warren Buffett, Charlie Munger, and their successors do all of the hard work.

If you study Warren Buffett for many years as I have, you will begin to notice that his stock picks follow a certain pattern. They are usually strong, well-known brands like Coca-Cola and Apple. He also likes to own financial companies like Bank of America, American Express, and Wells Fargo-- probably because these companies are highly leveraged and so make a lot of money during the good times. They also get bailed out by the government during the bad times.

It's important to remember that Buffett is the consummate insider. He's not just a folksy country bumpkin who sits around eating hamburgers and drinking Coke all day. When there is a sale of Goldman preferred shares with a 10% coupon, he gets the call. Not you or me.

That being said, there's one important lesson that we can all learn from Buffett's investing style. You want to own businesses that have good pricing power. This means that they can raise prices without losing customers.

When Coke decides to raise its prices by 10 cents per can, you probably don't even notice. But when your local gas station is priced 10 cents above its nearby competition, you will probably go to the competitor instead.

It's extremely difficult to get rich owning a price-competitive business. If you sell corn, oil, or generic clothing, you have a lot of competition, and your margins are razor thin.

On the other hand, if you have a strong brand or make a

unique product, you have less competition and higher margins. If someone wants an Apple laptop or a pair of Nike shoes, there's only one place to get them. That's why Apple and Nike can charge premium prices.

As Buffett says:

The single most important decision in evaluating a business is pricing power. If you've got the power to raise prices without losing business to a competitor, you've got a very good business. And if you have to have a prayer session before raising the price by 10 percent, then you've got a terrible business.

If you'd like to learn more about Warren Buffett's style of investment, check out my Amazon book Invest Like Warren Buffett here:

www.trader-books.com

6

VALUE INVESTING AND P/E'S

A t its most basic level, value investing is about buying something for less than it is worth. It is a very appealing strategy, since who doesn't like to get a great deal?

Many years ago, the famous investors Benjamin Graham and Warren Buffett made a lot of money using a very simple version of this strategy. They would look for a company that had net cash of $20.00 per share, and then try to buy shares of its stock for 15. In other words, they were trying to buy a dollar for 75 cents, or even less. Or they would just buy stock in a company that had a P/E of just 5 or 6.

P/E is a company's "price to earnings ratio." Let's say that a company's stock trades for $100 and that the company has earnings per share (EPS) of $6.50 over the last 12 months. We can calculate a trailing ("last 12 months") P/E ratio for that stock by simply dividing the stock price ("P") by the EPS ("E"), so 100/6.50 equals about 15.

We can say that this stock has a TTM P/E (trailing 12 months price to earnings ratio) of 15. Historically that is a pretty good average P/E for a stock or for the stock market as a whole.

Companies that are growing their revenues or earnings quickly ("growth stocks") tend to have P/E's above 25. So, for example, today Microsoft has a P/E of 27.70 and Amazon has a P/E of 79.

Companies that are in trouble often have P/E's below 10. So for example, today Bed Bath & Beyond (BBBY) has a P/E of 7.

Today people often confuse value investing with buying stocks with low P/E's. As we mentioned, that strategy worked well in the past when Warren Buffett was a young man, but it stopped working years ago.

Until you become an advanced investor, don't ever buy a stock with a P/E of 10 or less. It's just a bad hole to fish in. It is full of companies with giant debt loads, falling revenues, or outdated products like faxes and typewriters. And probably a few frauds as well. So stay away.

Another mistake that new investors make is buying "bargain stocks." In November 2015, the P/E of Bed Bath & Beyond (BBBY) hit a five-year low of 12.00, with the stock trading at around 60. When the P/E of a company hits a 5-year low, many analysts will recommend the stock as a "cheap stock."

Unfortunately, there is a very real tendency for cheap stocks to get even cheaper. By December 2018, the P/E of BBBY had fallen to just 5. And the stock had also crashed from 60 to 11.

Low P/E stocks are almost always pricing in future bad news. Don't ever expect to find good stocks in the bargain bin— unless perhaps you are at the end of a multi-year bear market. Even then, you are often better off buying a higher-quality company that has a higher P/E.

Let me give you a good example. In late 2009, you could buy shares of Blockbuster at a P/E of 2. Or you could buy shares of Netflix at a P/E of 26.

Guess which one turned out to be the better investment?

Blockbuster was trading at a P/E of 2 because its earnings were about to completely disappear. Netflix was trading at a multiple of 26 times its current earnings. But those earnings were about to explode upwards, as Netflix went on to steal almost every single Blockbuster customer.

In 2009, Netflix had earnings of $116 million. In 2018, Netflix had earnings of $1.2 billion. On 28 December 2009, Netflix had a market cap of roughly $3 billion. That means that if you bought a share of Netflix stock at the end of 2009, you were literally buying it at a future P/E of 2.50 ($3 billion divided by $1.2 billion).

As we mentioned before, if you are going to be a good investor, you need to learn how to think like Wayne Gretzky: you must "skate" to where earnings are going to be, not to where they have been.

If earnings are going to collapse, that P/E of 8 that you are paying might turn out to be a P/E of 100. If the company is headed for bankruptcy, common shareholders will be wiped out and the debt holders will own and control the company. That means that your stock is going to zero.

Paying a cheap price for a stock that is going to zero is never a good deal. We call these situations "value traps." They look like good values, but they turn out to be traps.

Yesterday's hot tech company is almost never a good deal when its share price has gone down a lot. Think Yahoo or Blackberry.

A low or falling stock price will make it difficult for the company to attract top talent. In this way, stocks don't just reflect a company's current prospects, but also play a role in determining a company's future prospects. A company with a high or rising stock price can use that stock to buy out competitors and pay for top talent. That's what Facebook did with WhatsApp and Instagram.

When you are just getting started, it is probably easier to trade growth stocks and momentum stocks. It is still possible to make money with value investing, but it requires in-depth knowledge of a company's fundamentals and the future state of its industry.

Technological change and changing consumer tastes (think, Millenials and Generation Z) are making it increasingly different to predict the future.

I hope that after reading this you will never buy a stock just because it is "cheap" or has a low P/E.

In the next chapter, I will teach you a much easier way to make money from stocks.

7

MAKE MONEY WITH GROWTH STOCKS

A growth stock is simply the stock of any company that is expected to rapidly grow its revenues or earnings.

Here's the first rule for trading growth stocks:

Ignore the high P/E.

Great companies that are rapidly growing will always trade at high P/E's. They might not even have any earnings. They might be losing a lot of money as they grow their market share, like Uber. They might even grow their market share for many years, before they turn on the profit spigot. That's what Facebook did. It grew the social network for many years, before finally turning on advertising.

Value investors will always tell you to stay away from companies with high P/E's or companies that are losing money. But if you do that, you will miss out on some of the greatest stock runs of all time. Microsoft, Starbucks, Home Depot, and Amazon all traded at very high P/E's for many years. Amazon still does. But these stocks have gone on to make their holders very rich.

Companies with high P/E's are pricing in high growth in future earnings. If it looks like growth is slowing or that those earnings may never appear, the market will trash the stock. That's why we always trade growth stocks with a clear stop loss.

If you are Warren Buffett investing in a mature company, the P/E does matter. If you are holding a growth stock for a few weeks or even months, nothing could matter less than the P/E.

Let me explain how I trade growth stocks:

I like to buy growth stocks that are hitting new 52-week highs, or even all-time new highs.

This may seem counter-intuitive to some. Isn't it risky to buy a stock that is at all-time new highs? Doesn't that mean that it has further to fall?

If you study the greatest growth stocks of the past, you will begin to notice that they spend a lot of time trading at all-time new highs. This makes sense simply because any stock that goes up a lot must (almost by definition) spend a lot of time trading at new highs.

Why would you ever want to miss out on one of these runs, simply because of a bias against high P/E's or a fear of buying a stock at an all-time new high?

There is, in fact, something wonderful and magical about a stock at an all-time high:

Every single holder of the stock has a profit.

By contrast, when a stock has crashed or is constantly hitting new 52-week lows, there are many investors and traders that have been left holding the bag. If the stock then tries to rally, these investors will be happy to get out by selling their shares at their break-even price. This provides constant downward pressure, and thus makes it more difficult for the stock to bounce back.

At a new all-time high, everyone who owns the stock has a profit. All of the losers are gone: they have already exited at a loss, or at their break-even price. At new highs, there are only happy traders and investors left.

Well, except for one group of traders that no one feels very much sympathy for: the short-sellers. These are traders who have shorted the stock (probably because "it has such a high P/E") and are betting that it will go down. At a new all-time high, everyone who has shorted the stock previously now has a losing trade on their hands. They are sweating bullets.

And there's only one thing that they can do to stem their losses: they must "cover" their shorts by buying back the stock. This buying only adds more fuel to the fire, driving the stock higher, and forcing out more short-sellers.

Meanwhile, a stock that has recently moved up a lot begins to be featured on CNBC and discussed by online commentators. This publicity brings in a new wave of buyers, who continue to drive the stock higher and make it hit even more new all-time highs.

I like to call these "rocket stocks." One way to find them is to constantly scour the list of stocks at 52-week highs or new all-time highs, which you can find here:

https://www.barchart.com/stocks/highs-lows/highs?timeFrame=1y

The next step is to look at a daily chart of each stock. I want to make sure that the stock is trading above its 50-day moving average; and that the 50-day moving average is above the 200-day moving average. That looks something like this:

This is a chart of The Trade Desk (TTD). The upper line is the 50-day moving average, and the lower line is the 200-day moving average. When a stock looks like this, you know that it is in an uptrend.

Never buy a growth stock if the stock is trading below its 200-day moving average, or if the 50-day moving average is trading below the 200-day moving average. If either of those two criteria are true, the stock is in a downtrend. There is nothing more dangerous than a growth stock in a down-trend. A growth stock might go up 300% over 3 years, and then fall 80-95% once it enters a downtrend. This can happen even with major companies. It happened to Cisco, Amazon, Crocs, and many other names.

If a growth stock is trading above its 50-day moving average, and the 50-day moving average is trading above the 200-day moving average, I am happy to be long. If the stock is trading at new 52-week highs or all-time highs, that's even better. If a stock gaps up to new highs after a strong earnings report, that can be a great buy signal. Due to an anomaly called "Post-Earnings-Announcement Drift" (PEAD), a stock that has gapped up like this will have a tendency to continue moving in the same direction for many days or even weeks. As a small investor, you can ride the wave, as larger institutional investors add to their positions over time and thus cause the stock to drift higher.

Sometimes I will wait for a consolidation to enter a stock. In this situation, you want to wait until the stock has been trading in a range-bound "box" above the 50-day moving average. I like to buy on a strong breakout (see the arrow in the image below) from this box, on above-average volume like this:

In a strong market, you can also buy every pullback to the 50-day moving average. This kind of trade has a great risk/reward ratio, since you can stop yourself out if the stock actually closes below the 50-day moving average.

There are a few more ways that we can put the odds in our favor with growth stocks.

Growth stocks perform much better when the entire stock market is also in an uptrend. If the SPY and QQQ are trading above their 50-day moving averages, and if their 50-day moving averages are above their 200-day moving averages, it is a good sign that the general stock market is in an uptrend. That uptrend will put the wind at our backs when riding growth stocks higher.

Also, I like to look for growth stocks that have a market cap of $5 billion or less. It takes a lot less money to push a $5 billion stock higher than it does a $500 billion market cap stock.

Many large mutual funds and hedge funds cannot even look at a stock if its market cap is less than $5 billion. If you can enter the uptrend early, when the stock has a market cap of less than $5 billion, you will be well-positioned if the stock trades higher. Once the stock reaches $5-10 billion, there is a whole new set of institutional buyers who will begin to take notice. As they purchase shares, it will drive the rocket stock even higher.

I also like to look for growth stocks, where the float is less than 20% of the total number of shares outstanding. The "float" is simply the number of shares of a stock that are actually available for trading.

To calculate the float, you just take the total number of shares outstanding and subtract all closely-held shares (those held by founders, employees, and original investors that are locked up and thus unable to be traded).

You can use this link to look up the float for any stock:

https://finance.yahoo.com/quote/LYFT/key-statistics

This link is set to LYFT, but you can use it to look up any stock's float, just by changing the ticker in the URL. The float and total shares outstanding are listed in the middle of the far-right column.

We can see from this link that LYFT currently has 273.1 million shares outstanding, but a float of only 14.68 million shares. The float is just 5% (14.68/273.1) of the total shares outstanding. This small float is quite typical of recent IPO stocks.

Stocks with small floats like LYFT are very easy to push around. Because there are so few shares available to trade, it's much easier for a small amount of buying or selling to move the stock up or down a lot. LYFT is an example of a stock that went down a lot after its IPO, due to its small float. But there are many growth stocks with small floats that will go up a lot if there is even a little bit of demand. For example, Twitter went public with a float of just 11.38%. Institutional and retail demand for the stock combined with the small float was enough to drive the stock from 45 to 74 in its first six weeks of trading.

I also like to look for growth stocks with a high short interest. "Short interest" is the quantity of shares that have been sold short by those who believe that the stock will go down. You can find a stock's short interest here:

https://finance.yahoo.com/quote/LYFT/key-statistics

Again, you can change the ticker in the URL to examine any other stock. Scroll down the far-right column, and you will see "Short % of Float." This is simply the number of shares that have been sold short, divided by the float (which we defined above). Some hated stocks will have a short interest as a percentage of float that is anywhere from 10-50%.

Now short sellers (traders who are betting that a stock will go down) are usually pretty smart. When a stock keeps hitting new 52-week lows and it has a high short interest, you want to stay away. Valeant (VRX) was a perfect example of this.

Short sellers are not, however, infallible. And when a stock with high short interest starts hitting new highs, short sellers will be forced to buy back their shorts, whether they were right about the company's fundamentals or not. When they do, the stock will often explode higher. High short interest is simply more fuel for a rocket stock's ascent. That's why if a growth stock is hitting new 52-week or all-time highs and it also has a "Short % of Float" that is greater than 10%, I get very interested. As the shorts get squeezed, a stock like this can sometimes move up 30% or more in a very short period of time.

We've spent a lot of time discussing when to buy a growth stock. That's usually the easiest part of the trade. Knowing when to sell (at either a loss or profit) can be more difficult. Here are some of the criteria that I like to use:

- Take profits when you are so excited and happy about your trade that you are losing sleep.
- Take profits if a stock moves up 100% in 2 weeks or less.
- Take profits when you are up 300% from your entry price.
- Take profits when all of your friends and CNBC begin to talk a lot about the stock. At this point, the trade has become crowded, and hence much more dangerous.
- Take profits if a taxi driver or barber tell you to buy the stock.
- Exit (with a profit or loss) when the stock closes below its 50-day moving average. Use this method to capture shorter moves.

- Exit (with a profit or loss) when the stock closes below its 200-day moving average. Use this method to capture longer moves.
- Exit (with a profit or loss) when the 50-day moving average crosses below the 200-day moving average. Use this method to capture longer moves.
- Use a 10-day or 20-day exponential moving average (EMA) as a trailing stop. Exit your position if the stock has a daily close below this EMA.
- You can also scale out of a profitable position. Sell 25% of your position every Monday for 4 weeks in a row, or something similar. That is a good way to lock in some profits, while still keeping some exposure to the stock in case it continues to move higher.

Just be sure to never add to a losing position. Pick a stop loss level when you enter the trade and stick to it. Only losers average losers. Rocket stocks go up fast, but they can also go down fast.

I usually like to risk no more than 1% of my trading account on each stock trade. Let's say that I am trading a $100,000 account. In that situation, I will risk only 1% of my account, or $1,000. If I enter the stock at 100 and the 50-day moving average is at 95, that means that my risk is 5 points on the stock (100-95). In that case, I should only buy 200 shares of stock. If I buy 200 shares of stock, and the stock falls 5 points, I will have lost $1,000 or just 1% of my total account size.

The key to making a lot of money is not losing a lot of money in the process. If my trading account goes down 50%, I will need to make 100% in my trading account just to get back to even. When you are first getting started trading, be sure not to dig yourself a hole like this. Keep your losses small and manageable, especially while you are still in the learning phase. It's OK to buy just 1 share of stock when you are testing out a new strategy (especially if you are using Robinhood and thus not paying any commissions).

8

MAKE MONEY WITH IPO'S

I'm often asked by new traders whether they should play IPOs. If you know what you are doing, IPOs can be a great way to make a lot of money. But if you don't, you will usually be left holding the bag.

Let me explain:

An IPO ("initial public offering") occurs when a formerly private company decides to take on outside investors. It does this by either having insiders (founders, company executives, venture capitalists, and other institutional investors) sell some of their shares to the public, or by having the company create new shares that can be sold to the public.

Those shares are then "listed" on a public stock exchange like the NYSE or Nasdaq, where anyone can buy or sell them.

IPOs allow insiders to cash out, while also raising money for a company to use to expand its operations.

There is usually a lot of hype and media coverage surrounding big IPOs (think Facebook, Alibaba, Lyft, and Uber). This hype helps to drum up buyers for the newly issued stock.

Unfortunately what often happens in an IPO is that insiders sell their shares to uninformed retail investors. It can be a giant transfer of wealth from the "dumb money" (you and me) to the "smart money" (insiders, VC's, etc). You will often get a flurry of IPOs at the end of a long bull market, as we saw in 1999-2000, and as we are now seeing in 2019.

So if you ever buy shares of an IPO, remember who you are buying from. You are buying from smart insiders who know everything about how the company operates, its strengths and weaknesses, and its future prospects.

The smart insiders might be selling their shares because they think that those future prospects are poor. Or they might just be selling so that they can buy their own private jet and Maui estate.

Either way, IPOs can be a great trading vehicle for the experienced trader. This is because IPOs usually have small floats and strong institutional support, at least for the first six months.

As we mentioned in the chapter on growth stocks, a small float means that not all of a company's shares are available to be publicly traded. A small percentage of an IPO's shares are allowed to be traded on the stock exchange, while the rest of the shares are "locked up" and can't be sold for at least 6 months.

Because there are so few shares available, it's much easier to move the stock up or down a lot. That's why Lyft (LYFT) crashed so quickly after its IPO. The company issued only 32.5 million shares out of a total of 273 million shares outstanding.

That's a very small float-- just 12% of its total shares were available to be traded. A few days after its IPO, short-sellers pounced on LYFT, driving it down from a high of 88.60 down to the high 40's.

The reverse can happen with a small float. PagerDuty (PD) IPO'd in April 2019 by selling only 9.07 million shares to the public, out of a total of 73.6 million shares outstanding. That's also a float of just 12%. The stock started trading in the high 30's, but quickly moved above 50.

Similarly GoPro (GPRO) ran from 30 to nearly 100 shortly after its IPO, before crashing back down. It now trades around 5.

Twitter (TWTR) ran from 45 to 73 shortly after its IPO, before crashing back down below its IPO price.

There are 2 ways to approach an IPO.

The first way is as a long-term investor. If you bought 1 share of Coca-Cola for $40 when it IPO'd in 1919 and held on to it, your position would currently be worth more than $15 million (assuming that you used all dividends that the stock paid you to buy more shares).

I wish that my grandfather had done that, but he didn't. If you bought shares of Walmart, Home Depot, Walt Disney, Starbucks, or Microsoft at the IPO and held on, you (or your grandchildren) are also very rich today.

Of course, if you bought shares of Webvan (an online grocery business) at its IPO in 1999, your investment is now worth zero. Webvan filed for bankruptcy in 2001.

It's hard to overpay at an IPO, if the company is going to be around in 30 years and massively expand its operations. But most companies do not grow up to become a Microsoft or Starbucks, so you cannot simply buy every IPO that comes out. There are just too many IPOs, and many of them are bankrupt just 5 years later.

To be a long-term investor in an IPO, you need to know something about the industry and also have a correct view of the company's future prospects. You then need to put the stock somewhere where you won't be tempted to actively trade it.

Even Coca-Cola's stock fell 50% in its first 12 months as a public company. Would you be able to hold on, watching your $10,000 investment become $5,000? That's the question that you need to ask yourself before you buy an IPO with the intention of holding it for the next 20 years.

There's a further complication. Companies used to go public (IPO) much earlier in their business lifecycle.

Amazon was founded in 1994, and went public in 1997 (just 3 years later). By contrast, Uber was founded in 2009, and did not go public until 2019 (10 years later). Amazon went public with a market cap of just $438 million. Uber went public with a market cap greater than $80 billion.

As companies stay private longer before having an IPO, the bulk of the gains go to the private market holders. Maybe Uber will go from $80 billion to $800 billion (making 10x on your money), but I doubt it. By contrast, public shareholders were able to profit from Amazon's rise from $438 million to over $900 billion (making 2052x on your money). If you bought Uber at the IPO as a long-term investor, you are probably the dumb money.

The second way to approach IPOs is from a trader's perspective. An IPO with a small float has the potential to go up or down a lot, which makes it a great trading vehicle.

In my experience, the more hyped an IPO is, the more difficult it will be to profit from it on the long side. However, I'm happy to short an over-hyped IPO, if the price action on it turns negative.

When I'm buying IPOs, I like to focus on more obscure companies, which I often find on this calendar of new IPOs:

https://www.nasdaq.com/markets/ipos/

When I want to trade a recent IPO, I usually just watch it for a couple of weeks, to get a better feel for how it is trading. If I feel that the S&P 500 is about to go down, I will often short a recent IPO that has a small float (assuming that I am able to borrow the shares to short). If the S&P 500 goes down 10%, a new IPO might go down 50-75%.

Likewise, if the S&P 500 has been going down for a few months and my indicators tell me that it is near a bottom, I will often buy a recent IPO with a small float. If the S&P 500 rallies 10% off its lows, a new IPO could go up more than 100%.

I also like to look for recent IPOs that are trading in a tight price range, with contracting volume. When the IPO breaks out of this range on expanding volume, I will often buy the breakout and hold for a couple of weeks, using a trailing stop. I did this with GPRO, which broke out from its range on 28 August 2014 at 48.90 and proceeded to run to the low 90's.

For these kind of trades, I usually use a 15-day exponential moving average (EMA) line as my trailing stop. If the stock closes below that line, I will immediately exit the trade. It's very important to trade IPOs with a stop loss and strict discipline. I've known too many people who bought an IPO for a trade, ignored their stop loss, and decided to hold onto the IPO as an investment. Many of those stocks ended up going to zero.

There is usually a "lockup" for IPOs. This means that insiders cannot sell any of their locked-up shares for the first 180 days of trading (this is why new IPOs often have a small float). After that, they are often free to dump most of their shares on the open market, which can sometimes cause the stock to go down sharply.

If you are trading an IPO, make sure that you are aware of when the lockup expires. Sometimes the expiration of a lockup will not move the stock significantly. Sometimes it will. That is why it is important to pay attention to the price action of a stock around its lockup.

Would you be interested in an online course that explores how to trade IPOs in more detail? If so, please contact me at matt@trader.university, and let me know. If there is enough demand, I would be happy to develop this course. There is much, much more to be said about trading IPOs.

9

HOW TO PROFIT FROM A STOCK THAT IS GOING NOWHERE

D id you know that there is a way to profit from a stock that is going nowhere?

Let's take stock XYZ which has been trading between 45 and 50 for the last year. Let's say that the stock is currently at 47.48. Now let's say that we don't expect the stock to rally from here, but we also don't expect it to crash. We believe that the stock will continue to bumble along between 45 and 50 for the next 4 months. It's currently the middle of April.

So we buy 100 shares of the stock at 47.48, and immediately sell one August 48.00 call option for 1.30. 100 shares of the stock costs us $4,748 (no commissions are charged if we use Robinhood.com). By selling an August 48.00 call option, we are giving someone the right to buy our 100 shares of XYZ stock from us at 48.00 anytime before the option expires in mid-August. In exchange we get to pocket $130.

We sold the call option for 1.30 and each call option is based on 100 shares of stock, so we multiply 1.30 by 100 to get $130. We get to keep this $130 no matter what happens to the stock. We are also entitled to any dividends that the stock pays while we're holding it.

If the stock is above 48 (the strike price of our call option) near expiration, the stock will be taken away from us at 48.00 and $4,800 will be deposited into our account (100 shares times 48.00). We paid only $4,748 for the stock, so that gives us a profit of $52 on our stock ($4,800 minus $4,748). Add that to the $130 that we pocketed from the call option, and you'll see we'll end up making $182.

You'll notice that in this example, we sold something (a call option) that we didn't already own. Don't worry about this for now.

If you decide to do a trade like this, just make sure that you use a "sell to open" order when selling the call option. If you decide to exit this position, you'll need to use a "buy to close" order to get rid of the call option. After this order is executed, you are free to sell your stock as you normally would. Just never sell your stock before you have exited the call position, or you'll risk getting yourself in trouble.

By now you've probably realized that this type of trade is

called a "covered call." You are short a call, but you are "covered" against a big loss by simultaneously owning the stock. For every call that you want to sell, you'll need to buy 100 shares of the underlying stock to make this work.

When entering a covered call position, always buy the stock first, then sell the calls at a strike price that is just above where you bought the stock. I usually like to go 3 to 4 months out when picking the expiration for my call option.

Covered calls are much easier than they sound. This is another one of those cases where you can learn more by actually doing it, than you can by just reading about it. As we mentioned before, covered calls work best when a stock is trapped in a trading range (i.e. trading sideways).

If you think that a stock is going to go up a lot, you don't want to sell calls against it, because that will cap your upside. If you think that a stock is going to go down a lot, you don't want to own it at all. You'll make money on the short call option, but lose a lot more if the underlying stock goes down a lot.

In this chapter, I have given you the short version of covered calls. For more in-depth coverage, you can check out my book Covered Calls Made Easy here:

www.trader-books.com

10

A DAY TRADING STRATEGY THAT ACTUALLY WORKS

Day trading refers to any trading strategy that involves buying and selling a stock on the same day. Strictly speaking, a day trader will never hold a position overnight. Lots of people try day trading and end up failing. That's why I want to give you a simple strategy that has worked well for me over the years.

This strategy takes advantage of a basic fact of market structure that we discussed in Chapter 1: it takes time for big players to enter and exit their positions. If a mutual fund or hedge fund is holding millions of shares of the stock XYZ, it cannot simply press a button to exit its position. If XYZ has just reported some very bad news in their latest earnings report, the fund is in a tough spot. It will take hours, days, or maybe even weeks for the mutual fund to exit its position, depending on how liquid the stock is.

And the same holds true for a stock that has just reported very good news in its latest earnings report. If a fund wants to open a new position in that stock, or to add to an existing position, it may take hours, days, or weeks.

The good news is that small traders like you and I can take advantage of these slow, lumbering giants. Once we see their footprints in a stock's price behavior, we can step in front of them and quickly execute our small order. Our small order will not push the stock in any direction. But the giant mutual fund's or hedge fund's large order will cause the stock to continue to move.

By jumping in front of a large institutional player, we can come along for the ride as the mutual fund or hedge fund continues to push the stock up with its buying, or down with its selling.

Let's start with an example. On 26 February 2019, the gaming company Sea Limited (ticker: SE) closed at 16.20. In the after-market hours, the company reported much better than expected earnings. How do we know that the earnings were better than expected? Because the next morning the stock opened 15% higher at 18.64. The stock continued to move higher for the rest of the day, closing at 21.99. In other words, after gapping up, the stock still moved up another 18% during the day.

Here's a day trading strategy that works to capture moves like this:

1. Find a stock that is gapping up on good news (like a better than expected earnings report).
2. Wait 15 minutes after the market's open, and note the stock's price at that time.
3. Put in a limit order to buy the stock at that price.
4. If your order is not executed in the next 15 minutes, cancel your order and walk away.
5. If your order is filled, hold on to the stock for the rest of the trading day, and then take profits a couple of minutes before the market closes that day.
6. Exit the stock early if it trades below the lowest price of that first 15 minutes of morning trading.

It's that simple. This strategy takes advantage of a stock's tendency to keep moving in the same direction of its morning gap, as large institutional players like mutual funds and hedge funds adjust their positions

What is a gap? It's simply when a stock moves up or down sharply, leaving a "gap" or empty space on the chart that separates it from its previous trading range. Here's a video about how I made $757 day trading Netflix using this strategy:

https://www.youtube.com/watch?v=koWQ5IoIoXk

11

FIVE HUGE MISTAKES THAT BEGINNERS MAKE

I get hundreds of emails every day from traders and investors, many of whom have just made one of the mistakes that I discuss in this chapter. If you can avoid these mistakes when you are just getting started, you will be way ahead of the pack and will also save yourself a lot of losses and misery. Write down these "5 Commandments" on a sticky note and put it on your computer screen:

1. **Don't buy stocks that are hitting 52-week lows.**
2. **Don't trade penny stocks.**
3. **Don't short stocks.**
4. **Don't trade on margin.**
5. **Don't trade other people's ideas.**

1. Don't buy stocks that are hitting 52-week lows.

We have already discussed this point, but it bears repeating, simply because so many new traders lose a lot of money trying to catch the proverbial "falling knife." In spite of what everyone will tell you, you are almost always much better off buying a stock that is hitting 52-week highs than one hitting 52-week lows.

Has a company that you own just reported some really bad news? If so, remember that there is never just one cockroach. Bad news comes in clusters. Many investors recently learned this the hard way with General Electric, which just kept reporting one bad thing after another, causing the stock to crash from 30 to 7. There is no such thing as a "safe stock." Even a blue chip stock can go down a lot if it loses its competitive advantage or the company makes bad decisions.

A cascade of bad news can often cause a stock to trend down or gap down repeatedly. If you own a stock that does this, it is often better to get out and wait a few months (or years) to reenter. Again, there is never just one cockroach.

Never buy a stock after you have seen the first cockroach. When a stock goes down a lot, it can affect the company's fundamentals as well. Employee and management morale will deteriorate, the best employees may leave the company, and it may become more difficult for the company to raise money by selling shares or issuing debt.

Conversely, when a stock goes up a lot, it can improve the

company's fundamentals. Employee and management morale will be high, everyone at the company will want to work harder, it will be easier to recruit new talent, and it will become easier for the company to raise money by issuing stock or debt.

If you stick to stocks that are trading above their 200-day moving averages, or that are hitting 52-week highs, you will do much better than trying to catch falling knives.

2. Don't trade penny stocks.

A penny stock is any stock that trades under $5. Unless you are an advanced trader, you should avoid all penny stocks. I would extend this by encouraging you to also avoid all stocks priced under $10.

Even if you have a small trading account ($5,000) or less, you are better off buying fewer shares of a higher-priced stock than a lot of shares of a penny stock.

That is because low-priced stocks are most often associated with lower quality companies. As a result, they are not usually allowed to trade on the NYSE or the Nasdaq. Instead, they trade on the OTCBB ("over the counter bulletin board") or Pink Sheets, both of which have much less stringent financial reporting requirements than the major exchanges do.

Many of these companies have never made a profit. They may be frauds or shell companies that are designed solely to enrich management and other insiders. They may also include former "blue chips" that have fallen on hard times like Eastman Kodak or Lehman Brothers.

In addition, penny stocks are inherently more volatile than higher-priced stocks. Think of it this way: if a $100 stock moves $1, that is a 1% move. If a $5 stock moves $1, that is a 20% move. Many new traders underestimate the kind of emotional and financial damage that this kind of volatility can cause.

In my experience, penny stocks do not trend nearly as well as higher-priced stocks. They tend to be more mean-reverting (Mean reversion occurs when a stock moves up sharply from its average trading price, only to fall right back down again to its average trading price). Many of them are eventually headed to zero, but they are still not good short candidates. Most brokers will not let you short them. And even if you do find a broker who will let you short a penny stock, how would you like to wake up to see your penny stock trading at $10 when you just shorted it at $2 a few days before? I learned that lesson the hard way. It turned out that I was risking $8 to make $2, which is not a good way to make money over the long term.

To add injury to insult, a penny stock might appear to be liquid one day, and the next day, the liquidity dries up and you are confronted by a $2 bid/ask spread. Or the bid might completely disappear. Imagine owning a stock for which there are now no buyers.

Stay away from all stocks under $10. Also stay away from trading newsletters that hawk penny stocks. The owners of these newsletters are often paid by the companies themselves to hype their stocks. Or they may take a position in a penny stock, send out an email telling everyone to buy it, and then sell their stock at a much higher price to these amateur buyers.

Watch the movie "The Wolf of Wall Street" if you'd like to see a famous example of the decadent lifestyle and fraud that often surround penny stocks. Viewer discretion is advised.

3. Don't short stocks.

If you are an advanced trader, feel free to ignore this rule. If you are not, I would seriously encourage you not to ignore this rule.

In order to short a stock, you must first borrow shares of the stock from your broker. You then sell those shares on the open market. If the stock falls in price, you will be able to buy back those shares at a lower price for a profit. If, however, the stock goes up a lot, you may be forced to buy back the shares at a much higher price, and end up losing more money than you ever had in your trading account to begin with.

In November 2015, Joe Campbell broke 2 of the 5 commandments. He first decided to trade a penny stock called Kalo-Bios Pharmaceuticals. To make things worse, he decided to short it.

When he went to bed that evening, his trading account was worth roughly $37,000. When he woke up the next morning, the stock had skyrocketed. As a result, not only had he lost all of the $37,000, but he now owed his broker an additional $106,000.

And there was no way out. If you owe your broker money, they can haul you into court and go after your house and savings.

Sometimes even the wealthiest investors can be wiped out by shorting a stock. During the great Northern Pacific Corner of 1901, shares of that railroad stock went from $170 to $1,000 in a single day. That move bankrupted some of the wealthiest Americans of the day, who had shorted the stock and were then forced to cover at higher prices.

If you do end up shorting a stock, remember that your broker will charge you a fee (usually expressed as an annual interest rate) to borrow the stock. In addition, if you are short a stock, you are responsible for *paying* any dividends on that stock (your broker will automatically take the money out of your account quarterly).

For all of these reasons, shorting stocks is clearly an

advanced and risky trading strategy. Don't try it until you've been trading for at least 5 years, and you have the financial stability to withstand a freakish upwards move in a stock.

And never short a penny stock. It's just not worth it.

4. Don't trade on margin.

In order to short a stock, you will need to open up a margin account with your broker, as Joe Campbell did. You'll also need a margin account in order to trade stocks using margin.

When you buy a stock on margin, it means that you are borrowing money from your broker, in order to purchase more shares of stock than you would normally be able to buy with just the cash sitting in your brokerage account.

Let's say that I have $10,000 in my margin account. Most brokers in the U.S. will allow me to go on margin to purchase $20,000 worth of stock in that account. What this means is that they are lending me an additional $10,000 (usually at some outrageous annual interest rate like 11%, which is what E*Trade currently charges) to buy more shares of stock.

If I buy $10,000 worth of stock and the stock goes up 10%, I've just made $1,000. But if I can increase the amount of stock that I'm buying to $20,000 using a margin loan, I will have made $2,000 on the same 10% move. That will mean that my trading account has just gone up by 20% ($2,000/$10,000).

Of course, if the stock goes down 10% and I'm on full margin, I will have lost 20% of my account value. Trading on margin is thus a form of leverage: it amplifies the performance of your portfolio both on the upside and the downside.

When you buy a stock using margin, the stock and cash in your trading account is held as collateral for the margin loan. If the stock falls enough, you may be required to add more cash to your account immediately (this is called "getting a margin call"), or risk having the broker force you to immediately sell your stock to raise cash. Often this will lead to your selling the stock at the worst possible time.

When you open up a new brokerage account and you are given the choice of a "cash account" or a "margin account," it's OK to pick "margin account." A margin account has certain advantages, such as being able to use the proceeds from selling a stock to immediately buy another stock without having to wait a few days for the trade to settle. If you never exceed your cash buying power in a margin account, you will never be charged fees or interest. In that way, it's quite possible to have a margin account, but never to go on margin.

If, however, you don't trust yourself, open up a "cash account." That way, you will never be allowed to trade on margin.

To learn more about how Robinhood handles margin, you can go here:

https://support.robinhood.com/hc/en-us/
articles/360026164112

5. Don't trade other people's ideas.

The first reason never to trade someone else's ideas is that they probably don't know what they are doing. If you get a hot stock tip from your neighbor or at the gym, it's best to ignore it. They probably have no idea what they are talking about.

Second, even if you get a really good and legitimate trading or investing idea from someone else, you will probably not have the conviction to hold on to it when the going gets tough. That conviction can only come from developing a trade idea yourself. When you have designed a trade, or researched an investment for yourself, you will have the conviction to hold on. You will also know where your stop loss is, in case the stock goes south. Have you noticed how hot stock tips never come with a recommended stop loss level?

Also, never place a trade based on something that you have just read in Barron's, Forbes, The Wall Street Journal, or have just seen on CNBC. Never buy a stock based on an analyst upgrade, or sell a stock based on an analyst downgrade.

I've seen analysts finally downgrade a stock only once it has fallen 50%. Analysts are lagging indicators. They tend to upgrade stocks that have already moved up, and downgrade stocks that have already moved down. There is also a strong selection bias among analysts. The best analysts get hired by hedge funds, and you never hear from them again. The worst analysts stay at the banks or brokerage houses, and continue to dispense their mediocre advice. Huge amounts of money have been lost by following their advice.

Should you even follow Warren Buffett's advice, as I suggested in a previous chapter? Yes, and no. His advice is definitely much better than a hot stock tip from your neighbor. On the other hand, if you listened to him religiously, you missed out on all of the great tech stocks of the last 20 years. He waited until Apple and Amazon were up many thousands of percentage points before finally purchasing them.

Anyone can learn to think for themselves in the stock market, and come up with their own trading and investing ideas. That is the goal behind all of my books and trading courses.

Rather than giving you a fish, I would much rather teach you how to fish for yourself. That is the path to true financial freedom.

12

INSIDER SECRETS OF THE STOCK MARKET

I n this chapter, I have listed some pearls of wisdom that I was unable to include in previous chapters. I also want to repeat some of the most important themes of this book, for the sake of emphasis.

Let me start by reminding you of one of the most important truths about the stock market:

Reaction to the news is always more important than the news itself.

And so, by extension:

Reaction to an earnings report is always more important than the earnings report itself.

It's almost always a bearish sign when a stock sells off after a good earnings report. If a stock that has had a big run-up falls on a good earnings report, it may be a sign that the uptrend is over.

The opposite is also true. When a stock still rallies after a "bad" earnings report, it is a bullish sign. It's also a bullish sign if the stock market rallies after a negative economic report.

Many people get stubborn and try to tell the stock market what to do. Smart traders listen to the market instead.

Just because you need to make money today does not mean that the opportunity will be automatically available. You must learn to be content with what the market is currently able to offer you.

Don't force a trade. Be patient, and wait for the fat pitch. If you can learn patience and discipline, the market will eventually reward you beyond your wildest dreams.

Focus on a few stocks, and get to know how they trade. Don't spread yourself too thin by trying to follow too many stocks.

If you have made a mistake, cut your losses quickly and move on. Never let a trade turn into a long-term investment. Don't average trading losses. Don't throw good money after bad. Never add to a losing position, but feel free to add to a position once it starts to make money.

The stock market is a discounting machine. That means that it takes all available information about a company and the economy and adjusts a stock's price accordingly. Sometimes it does a better job of this than other times. The stock market has a tendency to over-discount identified risks, and under-discount unidentified risks.

Whenever you keep hearing about a risk in the financial news, it is most likely already priced into a stock, or the stock market as a whole. It is the risks that you are not hearing anything about, or that seem absurdly unlikely, that can cause the most damage. If everyone is talking about something, it's almost always already priced into the market. That means that the stock has already moved to where it needs to be, based on all of the information that is currently available. As we mentioned before, to make money in trading or investing, you need to skate to where the puck is going to be, not to where it has already been.

A market that repeatedly fails to move higher will usually go down. The stock market (as well as individual stocks) will always search out our vulnerabilities, and move in such a way as to cause the maximum pain to the maximum number of traders.

In the short term, mass psychology rules the markets, not fundamentals or the economy. Improving company fundamentals and good economic news will often show up in stock prices before they show up in the headlines, which is why it is so important to pay attention to price action.

As long as the market is going up, and your stock is going up, don't be in a hurry to take profits. In order to win at this game, you will need to have some big winners. Don't choke them off too soon.

There is a seasonality to the stock market that we should not ignore. Although the 2 most famous stock market crashes both occurred in October (1929 and 1987), September has historically been the weakest month for the stock market. Average historical returns for June and August are also negative.

This has led to the famous expression "Sell in May and go away." Stock market returns from November through April have historically been much higher than stock market returns from May through October. This doesn't necessarily mean that you should sell all of your stocks and go to cash every May. But it does mean that you should be more cautious when trading during the summer months. Many traders and investors are at the beach, so liquidity is lower and volatility is higher.

If you are looking for a good long-term investment, buy a company that has the highest sales in its industry. So for home improvement, you want to own Home Depot; for fast food, McDonald's; for toothpaste, Colgate Palmolive; for payments, Visa; for smart phones, Apple; and for social media, Facebook. Once a business sells more than any other company in its industry, it becomes very difficult to compete with. There's no substitute for being #1 in your industry.

When all of the experts agree, then something different is going to happen in the market. The current conventional wisdom is always already priced into the market.

Here are some of my all-time favorite quotes about trading and the stock market.

George Soros: "It's not whether you're right or wrong that's important, but how much money you make when you're right and how much you lose when you're wrong."

John Maynard Keynes: "Markets can remain irrational longer than you can remain solvent."

Dennis Gartman: "The markets will return to rationality the moment that you have been rendered insolvent."

William Eckhardt: "Either a trade is good enough to take, in which case it should be implemented at full size, or it's not worth bothering with at all."

Ed Seykota: "Fundamentals that you read about are typically useless as the market has already discounted the price, and I call them 'funny-mentals.' I am primarily a trend trader with touches of hunches based on about twenty years of experience.

In order of importance to me are: (1) the long-term trend, (2) the current chart pattern, and (3) picking a good spot to buy or sell. Those are the three primary components of my trading. Way down in very distant fourth place are my fundamental ideas and, quite likely, on balance, they have cost me money."

Jim Rogers: "I just wait until there is money lying in the corner, and all I have to do is go over there and pick it up. I do nothing in the meantime. Even people who lose money in the market say, 'I just lost my money, now I have to do something to make it back.' No, you don't. You should sit there until you find something."

Bruce Kovner: "Whenever I enter a position, I have a predetermined stop. That is the only way I can sleep. I know where I'm getting out before I get in. The position size on a trade is determined by the stop, and the stop is determined on a technical basis."

Paul Tudor Jones: "Don't be a hero. Don't have an ego. Always question yourself and your ability. Don't ever feel that you are very good. The second you do, you are dead. My biggest hits have always come after I have had a great period and I started to think that I knew something."

Ed Seykota: "The key to long-term survival and prosperity has a lot to do with the money management techniques incorporated into the technical system. There are old traders and there are bold traders, but there are very few old, bold traders."

Bulls make money, bears make money, but pigs get slaughtered. A greedy trader who ignores his stop losses and other exit signals will give back all of his profits, and then some.

13

FROM SMALL BEGINNINGS TO GREAT WEALTH

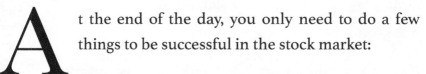t the end of the day, you only need to do a few things to be successful in the stock market:

Buy the strongest stocks that keep moving up. Add to your winners, get rid of your losers, and don't get too greedy.

Trading is actually quite simple. It's just not easy.

The good news is that anyone can learn to be a great trader.

All that is required is a good roadmap or mentor, discipline, and some good old-fashioned hard work.

Remember that 75% of new traders quit within the first 3 months. 90% of new traders quit within the first 6 months. If you can stick around long enough and keep learning, you will be successful at this game.

Never forget that. Anyone can learn to play this game.

If you have found this book to be helpful, be sure to check out my other books and courses here:

https://www.trader.university/

At Trader University, I provide traders and investors with a complete road map for all stages of their trading journey. Whether you are just getting started, or are already an advanced trader, you can learn a lot from my courses. I try to keep them as simple and practical as possible. No esoteric theories, no advanced math or trader's jargon— just the trading strategies that you need to start making money in the markets today.

If you have enjoyed this book, I would be very grateful if you could post an honest review on Amazon. All that you need to do is to **click here** (or go to www.trader-books.com) and then click on the correct book cover. Then click the blue link next to the yellow stars that says "customer reviews." You'll then see a gray button that says "Write a customer review"—click that and you're good to go.

If you would like to learn more ways to make money in the stock market, check out my other books on the next page.

ALSO BY MATTHEW R. KRATTER

Click here to buy this book on Amazon

Or simply go to www.trader.university and click on "Books".

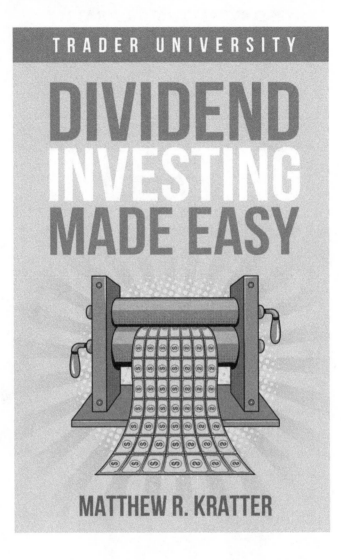

Click here to buy this book on Amazon

Or simply go to www.trader.university and click on "Books."

YOUR FREE GIFT

Thanks for buying my book!

To show my appreciation, I would like to send you a **FREE BONUS BOOK**, which contains 3 chapters:

- **"Interview with a Millionaire Trader"** (how he got started, and which trading strategies he is using today)
- **"Best Online Stock Screeners"** (my favorite stock scanners that I use to screen for momentum stocks and other trading set-ups)
- **"The Fastest Way to Grow a Small Trading Account"** (if you are trading less than $5,000, you won't want to miss this chapter)

To get your FREE copy of this book, tap here now:

>>>Tap Here to Get Your Free Bonus Chapter<<<

Or simply go to:

https://www.trader.university/beginners-guide-bonus

ABOUT THE AUTHOR

Hi there!

My name is Matthew Kratter.

I am the founder of Trader University, and the best-selling author of multiple books on trading and investing.

I have more than 20 years of trading experience, including working at multiple hedge funds.

Most individual traders and investors are at a huge disadvantage when it comes to the markets. Most are unable to invest in hedge funds. Yet, when they trade their own money, they are competing against computer algorithms, math PhD's, and multi-billion dollar hedge funds.

I've been on the inside of many hedge funds. I know how professional traders and investors think and approach the markets. And I am committed to sharing their trading strategies with you in my books and courses.

When I am not trading or writing new books, I enjoy skiing,

hiking, and otherwise hanging out in the Rocky Mountains with my wife, kids, and dogs.

If you enjoyed this book, you may also enjoy my other Kindle titles, which are available here:

http://www.trader.university

Just click on the tab that says "Books."

Or send me an email at matt@trader.university.

I would love to hear from you.

DISCLAIMER

While the author has used his best efforts in preparing this book, he makes no representations or warranties with respect to the accuracy or completeness of the contents of this book and specifically disclaims any implied warranties or merchantability or fitness for a particular purpose. The advice and strategies contained herein may not be suitable for your situation.

You should consult with a legal, financial, tax, health or other professional where appropriate. Neither the publisher nor the author shall be liable for any loss of profit or any other commercial damages, including but not limited to special, incidental, consequential, or other damages.

This book is for educational purposes only. The views expressed are those of the author alone, and should not be taken as expert instruction or commands. The reader is responsible for his or her own actions.

Adherence to all applicable laws and regulations, including international, federal, state, and local laws, is the sole responsibility of the purchaser or reader.

Neither the author nor the publisher assumes any responsibility or liability whatsoever on the behalf of the purchaser or reader of these materials.

Any perceived slight of any individual or organization is purely unintentional.

Past performance is not necessarily indicative of future performance.

Forex, futures, stock, and options trading is not appropriate for everyone.

There is a substantial risk of loss associated with trading these markets. Losses can and will occur.

No system or methodology has ever been developed that can guarantee profits or ensure freedom from losses. Nor will it likely ever be.

No representation or implication is being made that using the methodologies or systems or the information contained within this book will generate profits or ensure freedom from losses.

The information contained in this book is for educational purposes only and should NOT be taken as investment advice. Examples presented here are not solicitations to buy or sell. The author, publisher, and all affiliates assume no responsibility for your trading results.

There is a high risk in trading.

HYPOTHETICAL OR SIMULATED PERFORMANCE RESULTS HAVE CERTAIN LIMITATIONS.

UNLIKE AN ACTUAL PERFORMANCE RECORD, SIMULATED RESULTS DO NOT REPRESENT ACTUAL TRADING. ALSO, SINCE THE TRADES HAVE NOT BEEN EXECUTED, THE RESULTS MAY HAVE UNDER-OR-OVER COMPENSATED FOR THE IMPACT, IF ANY, OF CERTAIN MARKET FACTORS, SUCH AS THE LACK OF LIQUIDITY.

SIMULATED TRADING PROGRAMS IN GENERAL ARE ALSO SUBJECT TO THE FACT THAT THEY ARE DESIGNED WITH THE BENEFIT OF HINDSIGHT. NO REPRESENTATION IS BEING MADE THAT ANY ACCOUNT WILL OR IS LIKELY TO ACHIEVE PROFIT OR LOSSES SIMILAR TO THOSE SHOWN.